BUSINESS 365

Daily Inspiration for Creativity,
Innovation and Business Success

Tips, Ideas, Principles & Strategies

Victor Kwegyir
Entrepreneur, International Business Consultant,
Coach & Speaker

BUSINESS 365

Copyright © 2020 by Victor Kwegyir

Published by
Vike Springs Publishing Ltd.
www.vikesprings.com

First Edition
ISBN - 978-1-9998509-8-2 – Ebook
ISBN - 978-1-9998509-9-9 - Paperback

PATHWAY TO BUSINESS SUCCESS SERIES

Printed
In the United Kingdom and
the United States of America

To request Victor for speaking engagements, interviews, mentoring, proposal writing, ghost writing and publishing, coaching or consultation services, please send an email to:
admin@vikesprings.com

Victor's books are available at special discounts when purchased in bulk for promotions or as donations for educational and training purposes.

LIMIT OF LIABILITY/ DISCLAIMER OF WARRANTY

DEDICATION

To all the entrepreneurs, business owners and aspiring entrepreneurs going after their dream daily with persistence and consistently. It might be daunting and potentially take longer than you thought but the success and experience will be worth the struggle.

INTRODUCTION

Entrepreneurship is a path many have travelled on and continue to do so. While a great number have succeeded at building their own business, many others have not. And even for the many who survive the curve, there are times of highs and lows. To survive such lows, we must draw inspiration from an inner store, from your faith, or from others and resources such as this book.

Business 365 offers you something to inspire, as well as help you as a companion for each day of every calendar year. And it is my hope that at no point in a calendar year will you find yourself with nothing to inspire, motivate and or challenge you as you continue to press on to achieve your goals and attain greater success in your industry.

Stay the course. Keep the focus.

Day 1

Never be distracted by another person's success. Focus on your unique path and timeline to success. That is when productivity increases, true efficiency is maximised and dreams get fulfilled.

Day 2

You don't go into business just based on motivation. You go into business with the right tools, strategies and professional advice. Anything less than that and you will be found wanting.

Day 3

The human mind is unbelievably rich with great ideas and possibilities. Employ it, feed it, challenge it, and it will work wonders for you.

Day 4

Leadership is not in the position you are in but in the values you stand for, the principles you live by and how you conduct yourself, both privately and publicly.

Day 5

Lessons can only be learnt by going through the process. Not outside it, around it, through someone else or by paying your way out of it.

Day 6

Value is often associated with how much you want something. If you really want it, you are more inclined to place a higher value on it. The opposite equally applies.

Day 7

Your greatest asset is the way you think. Not your skills, resources or the position you occupy. Because with the right mindset, you can turn any situation into greater success.

Day 8

Planning on a daily basis still counts. Just make sure you prioritise. Doing things anyhow without prioritising will steal away your most valuable asset – your time.

Day 9

Dreams give birth to passion and passion produces action. Your work ethic, consistency and determination deliver excellent results.

Day 10

A lesson learnt is better than a mistake never made.

Day 11

A teachable spirit or
attitude is among the
greatest assets one
can possess in life and
in business.

Day 12

Let the prize be your source of motivation, not just the goal. Aim higher.

Day 13

To avoid the process is to deny yourself the rewards. Postponing the process can rob you of the time you get to enjoy the rewards.

_____

_____

_____

_____

Day 14

A dedicated approach to business is an attitude that when you master it, can enable you to succeed at anything in life.

Day 15

Don't settle for anything less than your value. Know your price, and refuse to allow others to set it for you.

Day 16

A poverty mentality makes you place less value on time. You don't appreciate it yourself and have no respect for other people's time.

Day 17

If you believe you are a great prospect, then you will be a great prospect. Often, by simply showing up and taking action, we confirm that belief. Because the more you practice something, the more your skills improve and the better your results will be.

Day 18

Information makes
you knowledgeable.
Discernment makes you
wiser.

Day 19

If your vision doesn't make sense to you, your vision won't make sense to the investor.

Day 20

Successful people don't just work hard, they work smart. And that, my friend, is the basis of strategy!

Day 21

When it comes to high-level decisions and quick fixes, sometimes shortcuts work out, but you may lose the chance to find other problems, identify other solutions or discover different ways to improve.

Day 22

Successful people make time for people, activities and events that matter to their journey.

Day 23

Once you find your
purpose, it is too powerful
and addictive to let go.

Day 24

Quality is a result of attention to detail. Until you give every aspect due attention, you can never exceed the average.

Day 25

Excellence has no limits because there is always room for improvement.

Day 26

Knowledge can be exclusive, but wisdom is never exclusive.

Day 27

Starting a business is an investment. And until you see it that way, it will be a challenge to manage your expectations.

Day 28

Success always comes to those who do it right.

Day 29

Get your thinking right, and the rest is history.

Day 30

The greatest mistake or limitation of an individual is not knowing what you want in life, relationships or business.

Day 31

Until you put a value on what you need, it will never become yours.

Day 32

The truth is, what you sell
as a business must be of
good value if it is going
to be the customers'
preferred choice over
anything else that exists in
the market.

Day 33

The value of your product or service dictates the amount of time and resources you need to market it to your prospects.

Day 34

By all means network. However, what counts is the quality of the network. Never underestimate that. It makes a huge difference.

Day 35

When you lose your identity, you lose your sense of reasoning. Define who you are, and your focus will be as clear as ever.

Day 36

No number of lectures or education will deliver to you what going through the process can teach you.

Day 37

You are never short of passion when you are an original.

Day 38

You can never grow above what you are consciously or unconsciously exposed to.

Day 39

You may be able to fake love, but you can never fake passion. Because it is a driven inner force. And it is necessary for your business success.

Day 40

You should think through things thoroughly and see the impact on the quality of your output. You will shock yourself.

Day 41

To shift the responsibility
of your process is to gift
others with your potential
rewards.

Day 42

If you don't control your mind and steer it right, it will not be productive enough to serve your purpose. Take charge now.

Day 43

The difference between price and value is that price is the amount of money a customer pays for a product and/or service. Value, on the other hand, is the customer's perceived benefits of that product and/or service.

A value for money promotion strategy is not just dependent on advertising on any available platform but a platform available to and accessed by the target customer. A successful advertising campaign strategy aims at the best combination of the two.

Day 45

When discipline is your
friend, your journey to
the top becomes shorter.
Because everything else
hinges on it.

Day 46

The process is what produces great leaders and influencers. There is no great leader or icon in history without a story.

Day 47

The process is what separates boys from men and girls from women.

Day 48

The process is your friend and your best bet to achieve greater heights and success.

Day 49

The process will always cause pain, but the rewards make it worth it. Never despise your process!

Day 50

Your process is unique to you and your divinely ordained assignment. Many avoid it, thus losing out in life.

Day 51

Think before you talk to ensure what you are saying makes sense. Or else you risk embarrassing yourself, if not lose a client or significant business contract/deal.

Day 52

If you don't restrict who has access to you, even the unqualified become a priority. Be smart and take charge.

Day 53

If you keep excusing mediocre standards, you will struggle to exceed even your own past performance.

Day 54

If you live by your feelings and for convenience, you will never accomplish anything of significance in this life.

Day 55

Discipline is the mother of effort. If you master it, even the most difficult of roads to the top will become bearable.

Day 56

Being conscious of other people's time and space and thoughtful enough to appreciate it when given access is a huge blessing.

Day 57

Being courteous and well-mannered is "gold" in business. All that counts is knowing how to say thank you, please, sorry, sir, ma'am and being nice and kind.

Day 58

Have the ability to say or do anything but exercise the maturity to not do it. This is higher level living.

Day 59

Being respectful and confident when you can be otherwise because of age, status or influence is simply awesome! Try it.

Day 60

Being responsible is attractive. Do not live by excuses, but be responsible for your actions, meet obligations and earn trust.

Day 61

Being trustworthy
and having integrity is
an enviable platinum
combination that always
breaks barriers in the end.

Day 62

The process is real! There is work to do, mistakes to make, risks to take and success to achieve—if you don't faint first!

Day 63

Until you partner your brain with your emotions, you won't make the best decisions and cannot accomplish much in life.

Day 64

A poverty mentality makes
you feel like you know it
all. You see speaking to an
expert as a waste, rather
than an investment.

Day 65

If you don't want any opposition in life, please do NOT do anything. Because as soon as you sign up for any meaningful project or goal, you will attract some challenges. The greater the impact on the well-being of society, the greater the challenge will be. But don't fret, you can overcome it.

Day 66

When you lose the art of respecting what others bring to the table, you lose the art of learning. Because wisdom does not come from just one person.

Day 67

When you take 'access' to mean 'familiarity', you end up losing it all, including potential opportunities. It pays to learn to use your 'access' respectfully.

Day 68

You don't lack help when you give it freely and consistently. Often, even before you ask, it is offered to you. Be kind and caring.

Day 69

Entrepreneurs who pay for expert advice do so because they are smart enough to know ROI (return on investment) is guaranteed.

Day 70

No one succeeds in business all by themselves. Even the experts invest in seeking relevant knowledge. Either spend time researching and learning about your business or hire someone who has done it to teach you.

Day 71

How much you are willing to invest in business advice tells me how serious you are about your success. There is always something new to learn from the right person or source.

Day 72

Until you are willing to budget a good amount for quality advice as you are on materials, you are not ready to succeed. Make provisions for expert advice; it will be worth it.

Day 73

Irrespective of the challenges, the process will become exciting if the destination is real enough to you!

....

....

....

....

....

Day 74

Personal hygiene, keeping your environment clean, being conscious of it, looking good and smelling good are great characteristics of a leader.

Day 75

Plan so that your exposure to negative outcomes is kept to the barest minimum and positive outcomes become the norm!

Day 76

To enjoy a good life, you must envision it, dream it, desire it and recreate it over and over again in your mind. You must also plan it, sacrifice for it, expect it, see it and experience it.

Day 77

Your value is in the price you had to pay and the choices you had to make to get to where you are now.

Day 78

You do not grow and become successful by default. You have to learn and take sound advice along the way.

Day 79

Your growth will be slow until you learn to value the right knowledge and the right strategies from the right sources.

Day 80

You will never be ready to take your place until you are willing to grow into where you are going.

Day 81

Don't just desire to succeed, prepare to handle success when you get there!

Day 82

Character always has the last word. What does your character say about you

Day 83

If you don't take the step of faith/risk on your ideas and concepts, you will always end up complaining and envying those who act on theirs to make things happen.

Day 84

If you don't commit to
identifying your unique
strengths or abilities,
working on turning them
into a business or using
them to bless others, you
will become a slave to envy.

Day 85

You always have a choice. You can either remain ignorant or be knowledgeable and up to date in life, both of which come at a cost, although the latter has immense benefits if you do something with what you learn from it.

Day 86

Until you learn to master distractions, your attention will always be directed at what others are doing, keeping you from focusing on your target.

Day 87

If you lack endurance, you can never build anything worth applauding.

Day 88

Purpose attracts distractions and detractors like nothing else. It needs deliberate and purposeful guarding to stay on course.

Day 89

The greater the destiny, the
more mentoring you need,
including staying under
some kind of leadership
and authority to serve and
learn. Destiny, and learning
as a servant first; they work
together.

Day 90

A society where people are ridiculed for going after their bold dreams ends up becoming ridiculed itself!

Day 91

The value of a question is in the answer it generates. Give it a bit more thought if you expect the right answer.

Day 92

Have a healthy relationship with your online (social media) presence. Never allow it to distort your personality or steal your sense of discretion.

Day 93

Have the ability to keep some things private, no matter how tempting it may be. Because once you put it out there, it's there forever. Balance is key to your peace.

Day 94

Success rarely starts outside the realm of a person's thinking faculty. It is why you must be willing to renew your mind and engage it productively.

Day 95

Attaining a different level of success without updating your knowledge base or changing environment is an uphill task.

Day 96

If your mindset is wrong, very little will go right. If it is right, then it is gold. Because you will eventually get to where you want to be.

Day 97

The why of going into business makes a difference. If your why is pure and authentic, you stand a higher chance of success.

Day 98

A poverty mentality makes you place less value on knowledge. You always have a reason for not investing in yourself.

Day 99

Time is a major factor.
Expecting too much too
soon can kill your drive.
Allow the time factor to
work for you.

Day 100

Excellence opens doors
and establishes you,
whichever way you turn.

Day 101

The cost of producing a plan is always significantly lower than the cost of groping around in the dark with no plan.

Day 102

Not planning is simply a lack of strategy in business. It is too expensive to overlook.

Day 103

Planning before starting anything and a periodic review of strategy as you build, is bound to save you significant time and resources.

Day 104

The right body of knowledge offers you a solid basis for strategy. Mix that with action and success will be yours.

Day 105

Until you begin to
truly value knowledge,
progressive change will be
hard to come by.

Day 106

You attract opportunities when you are prepared. Your success is tied to taking advantage of such opportunities.

Day 107

If it is worth the time, it is worth giving it your all.

Day 108

Never compromise on your integrity and good name, because everything else hinges on it. Ultimately, it is your brand.

Day 109

The truth about life is that life is not fair. It only gives you what you fight for and not what you qualify for.

Day 110

If your quest to prosper is not aimed at honouring God as a believer, then it seems you've missed the point of it all.

Day 111

Giving creates room for receiving. It also endears you, even before your haters. They might not acknowledge it, but they will feel it.

Day 112

It is better to see the customer as 'doing you a favour' by choosing you above the competition and patronizing your products and services rather than the other way around.

Day 113

One of the ways you can kill jealousy is by going crazy celebrating other people's success without thinking twice about it.

Day 114

You can also kill jealousy by identifying your gift. Commit to perfecting your gift and use it to solve problems continuously.

Day 115

When you are busy
helping others and solving
problems, the sense of
fulfilment can overwhelm
you until you have no room
to be jealous.

Day 116

Although it can be excruciating, challenges are promotional stepping stones to the next level.

Day 117

You can live your dreams if you remain focused on the treasure…not the trouble.

Day 118

A higher value breakthrough demands a higher quality mindset.

Day 119

A higher value breakthrough demands a higher quality process and preparation.

Day 120

A higher value breakthrough demands a higher quality discipline and lifestyle.

Day 121

A higher value breakthrough demands a higher quality sacrifice.

Day 122

This is no secret folks, but the quality of your network influences the value of your net worth in the long run.

Day 123

Loving wisdom and not hungering for knowledge is impossible. Because knowledge feeds wisdom.

Wisdom enables you to appreciate the little things that come together for the big things to thrive.

Day 125

Planning gives birth to strategy. Without a plan there is no strategy, and without strategy there is no effective and efficient execution.

Day 126

Ordinary men don't produce outstanding success because it always takes a bit of madness to become outstanding.

Day 127

Planning offers you an advance walk-through, enabling you to better assess the cost, time, skills, and commitment you need to make your dream/vision/goal a reality.

Day 128

Wisdom is given by God, but the increase of it comes from your hunger and commitment to search for more. Knowledge adds flavour to it.

Day 129

Wisdom says do what is necessary now, but always consider its impact on your tomorrow.

Day 130

What is right always wins in the end. Because that is how lasting results are produced.

Day 131

Wisdom will always choose what is right over what is convenient. The result is lasting success.

Day 132

Wisdom and intelligence are not the same. Intelligence comes from what is taught. Wisdom comes from above and supersedes intelligence.

Day 133

Your mindset is the epicentre of all you do. You must seriously renew and inform it. It determines what you attract.

Day 134

Everyone has a price! Either you set it, allow others to set it for you or you allow your circumstances to determine it for you. Set your price!

Day 135

Everyone has value! Either you state your value and affirm it by your output, or hand over permission for people to determine it for you.

Day 136

Everyone has standards, whether they are stated or not, or even defined! Either they are low or high, or you are completely ignorant as to what they are.

Day 137

Not everyone whose opinion you respect will always get it right. They can be wrong sometimes. Take responsibility to make final decisions, and if it fails, own up to it and move on.

Day 138

Until you learn to concentrate your efforts in line with your purpose, you will not fulfil destiny.

Day 139

Success at anything starts in the mind. Just don't let it end as a beautiful image of what it could be. Work at it to bring the imagery into reality.

Day 140

In life, you must qualify whose opinion counts and whose opinion doesn't count. Until you do that, you will struggle to make significant progress. Because not everyone's opinion counts on the same level.

Day 141

Being principled does not give you permission to be insensitive, harsh or heartless. After all, at times you miss yourself!

Day 142

There is always something to be done about your situation. The least you can do is ask for help to give birth to your dream and get back on your feet. Do not surrender to the victim mentality and live your life always begging just to survive. If you must beg, beg only to help you bring forth that dream. Be smart!

Day 143

It is easy to make decisions when you are principled. Because your boundaries are often set already, and you do only that which is right.

Day 144

A principled person respects other people's principles and actually celebrates them, never forget that.

- - - - - - - - - - - -
- - - - - - - - - - - -
- - - - - - - - - - - -
- - - - - - - - - - - -
- - - - - - - - - - - -

Day 145

Most businesses fail, not because of the 'big picture' but because of the little things that were given less attention or completely ignored.

Day 146

A smart entrepreneur will address all the possible pitfalls to improve his or her chances of success significantly.

Day 147

Businesses fail when the entrepreneur lacks direction and focus. Many people get easily distracted because they lack clearly-defined goals and direction.

Day 148

When a person is hungry to make a difference they are often less bothered about how opportunities are presented to them.

Day 149

Businesses fail when
the entrepreneur lacks
appreciation for customers.
It is dangerous not to know
customer psychology and
how it works for you.

Businesses fail when the entrepreneur can't manage expectations. An inability to manage expectations can be a huge drawback to your success.

Day 151

Businesses fail when the entrepreneur does inadequate research. Poor research can cause you to struggle to define your target market clearly. This is a huge problem.

Day 152

Businesses fail when the entrepreneur lacks appreciation for knowledge. Without knowledge, you waste time and increase costs significantly

Day 153

Businesses fail when the entrepreneur lacks appreciation for good strategy. Until you have one everything you do is trial and error. Very costly!

Day 154

Businesses fail when the entrepreneur fails to plan. If you don't plan, you won't be able to accurately gauge the cost and what running your business entails.

Day 155

Businesses fail when the entrepreneur has the wrong mindset. If your thoughts on business are wrong, it won't take long before the struggles begin to bite.

Day 156

Working hard still counts. Just add strategy and working smart to it if you genuinely want to become successful.

Day 157

Marketing daily still counts! Just make sure you focus on the right segment of your market to get the right results. Consistency is the key in maximising returns on your marketing budget.

Day 158

Business values and strategy still count! Just make sure you don't sacrifice long-term gains for short-term benefits. It always comes back 'calling'.

Day 159

Business coaching still counts! Just make sure you are willing to learn and value it enough to act on it. Value is often associated with how much you are willing to pay for the coaching.

Day 160

Consistency with hard work always pays. The road to success is not as smooth as it is to read.

Day 161

If you are serious about it then prepare! Plan! And save for it. Above all, invest in yourself.

Day 162

No one becomes better at something by partial commitment. You are either all in or all out.

Day 163

Become determined to invest in yourself and your dream. Engage qualified experts, not anyone parading as one with no experience or track record.

Day 164

Keep your focus, don't be distracted by what everyone else is doing. Be persistent and consistent, with a good strategy.

Day 165

Quality is a product of attention to detail. Until you give every aspect due attention, you can never exceed the average.

Day 166

It is said that 'money makes the world go round'. If that is the case, then get yours and enjoy the ride.

Day 167

A smart entrepreneur
ensures their integrity
is always intact because
it pays huge dividends
in the end.

Day 168

It stands to reason that when you enjoy what you do, it fuels your quest to become better at it, and to deliver excellence.

Day 169

You don't have to be rich to have high standards. Standards help you build the right foundations to create wealth.

Day 170

High standards contribute
to our success and rise
to greatness. Nothing
significant is achieved
without them. Never forget
that.

Day 171

To grow and become successful is not by default. You have to learn from experts and apply their advice to experience it.

Day 172

When we face a challenge, we should not just throw in the towel and move on. Often, a little adjustment, adaptability, or just moving things around a bit to get a clearer picture from feedback does the trick, giving you the breakthrough you desire.

Day 173

No one succeeds in business all by themselves. If you can, then it's probably a hobby. Invest in seeking relevant knowledge.

Day 174

Until you ask for more, life only gives you the crumbs. The meat is preserved for those who answer the right questions.

Day 175

Some go through life with an appreciation that there is more to it than we see. That is how achievers are born.

Day 176

Some people strut through life with no desire to understand what it is all about, exiting without having made any defined impact. Don't be one of them.

Day 177

It's not just about having high standards, but purpose. Because your purpose should determine the standards you live by.

Day 178

Grateful people give. It is among their greatest traits. They see giving as an opportunity and not a pain to endure.

Day 179

Until you are consistent in your persistence, you can't receive anything worth celebrating.

Day 180

Values cannot be hidden, no matter how hard you try. They are seen by others in every action we take and every decision we make.

Day 181

Discerning customers always look for value, not the cheapest price available

Day 182

One of the greatest discoveries in life is knowing who you are, what you've been created for and what it takes to accomplish it.

Day 183

You cannot afford to not fail when it comes calling, because failure offers you an opportunity to innovate.

Day 184

Keep your eyes on the ball
if the object of being in the
game is to score goals.

Day 185

Honesty is not leaving an iota of doubt in a person's mind about your true intentions. It is being transparent right from the onset.

Day 186

If others have to keep figuring out what you mean, want or where your loyalty lies, then there is an issue with your words and actions.

Day 187

Honesty is not demanded before it manifests. It announces itself right from the start, before there is ever the need to question it.

Day 188

Honesty may take longer to deliver on a promise, but it will surely be delivered. Honesty will always make good on the promise.

Day 189

Honesty may cost much more than anticipated, but it will never be abandoned. It will eventually deliver!

Day 190

To succeed, you need to find your authenticity, and to become really successful, you need to find your own voice.

Day 191

Until you are ready to think in value rather than cost, you are not ready to grow, let alone become successful!

Day 192

The amount of resources you are willing to spend on preparation and planning says everything about how much faith you have in your dream!

Day 193

Your success rate has a lot to do with what you value most and are willing to spend time, expert knowledge and resources on.

Day 194

Become comfortable with asking 'What is in it for me' Even if it's not monetary returns. Never shy away from it.

Day 195

When confronted with long-term gains as opposed to short-term windfall, think. Long-term gains often get my vote!

Day 196

Successful people know that their time is invaluable. Time is an asset, and you must protect it.

Day 197

Success only comes to those who work hard and smart on the dream and remain consistent at it. There is no other way around it.

Day 198

Purpose is too powerful and addictive to let you go once you find it.

Day 199

If you don't love what you do, you wear out in no time.

Day 200

In life, until you finish exploring you, you cannot give up on you. It is important to know what you are made of, both internally (inner gifting and capabilities) as well as externally (skills and activities) to make sense of the true you.

Day 201

No one has enough time in this life. People make time for what they care about or what is important to them. It is always an issue of choice, rather than the number of hours available.

Day 202

Faith is your greatest anchor in the storm. It is your best bet of surviving it and going on to become a success against all odds.

Day 203

It is not faith until you believe that what hasn't happened yet is your reality, and it is only a matter of time until you will experience full manifestation.

Day 204

Faith makes you work. It gives you the belief to take steps. It is not faith if it doesn't move you to act.

Day 205

Faith is the greatest motivator. To have it makes you not give up easily. You easily become demotivated when it is missing.

Day 206

Never rush anyone to sign up for your vision. To give you total commitment, they must fully appreciate the depth, meaning and the requirements of the journey ahead.

Day 207

Never sign up for an
assignment, project or
program that you don't
have a full understanding of.
You risk signing away your
integrity and values. Ask
questions until you get it.

Day 208

Never take anyone at face value or allow titles to deceive you. Some need time to prove who they really are, because they may not even know who they really are themselves, or what they are capable of doing until they are put to the test.

You fall victim to scams easily when you focus on the money instead of the problem a business solves. Real businesses solve problems.

Day 210

In life, in business and in your career, someone or something has to introduce you to your next level of promotion, platform or breakthrough. The question is, what will they/it say about you and your abilities

----

Day 211

Entrepreneurs are
self-motivators and
hardworking!

Day 212

Entrepreneurs are go-getters. They don't wait for perfect conditions!

Day 213

Entrepreneurs are action oriented. They just can't be idle!

Day 214

Entrepreneurs don't give up easily. They have a never-quit attitude!

Day 215

Entrepreneurs are focused and visionary, with a singular desire to make a lasting impact!

Day 216

Entrepreneurs are driven by the dream and the rewards!

Day 217

Entrepreneurs are often very passionate about what they do and the impact they make on people's lives!

Day 218

Entrepreneurs are creators
and agents of innovation in
the world!

Day 219

Wherever entrepreneurs are encouraged and celebrated, society prospers much faster!

Day 220

Entrepreneurs make things happen that change not only their own lives but the lives of many others!

Day 221

Entrepreneurs are chief servants; they get down dirty and do not just concern themselves with being a boss and issuing instructions to others!

Day 222

Entrepreneurs spread the wealth around best, offering anyone the opportunity to better their life!

Day 223

Entrepreneurs are employers, helping national governments address the unemployment rates in any nation. Smart governments know it and create the enabling environment!

Day 224

Entrepreneurs are solution-minded providers in the face of many global problems!

Day 225

Entrepreneurs are risk takers often ready to embrace their failures, learn from them and try again!

Day 226

It is better to step out and
fail than to sit clutching
a few eggs which may
not remain forever. Take
calculated risks.

Day 227

The greatest barrier to your progression and success in life is the way you think.

Day 228

A business has a right to exist and profit from its operations, as long as it continues to solve customers' problems, stays relevant and offers sufficient value.

Day 229

The easiest way to come up with a business idea is to look for a problem to solve. And if it matches up with your passion, skill set or experience, that is even better.

Day 230

Keep dreaming, but you've got to wake up to make it happen.

Day 231

Failure gives you are opportunity to consider better options. Don't throw in the towel just yet!

Until you believe in your dream, you can't imagine it; until you imagine it, you can't see it; and until you see it, you can't possess it.

Day 233

Doing is always a better option than just trying because doing gets you more focused, and there is no room to give up. Whereas trying hands you the choice to give up anytime.

Day 234

More is accomplished in life by a person who is guided by principles than by one who relies on their will. When your will fails, let your principles prevail because you stand a better chance of making a success of your dream.

Day 235

It is the battles you choose to fight that determine how much you can accomplish and how far you can go in this life.

Day 236

Entrepreneurship is not just hard work and long hours, but smart work and belief in yourself and your ideas. That is what delivers results.

Day 237

Successful entrepreneurs adapt. PERIOD!

Day 238

God worked six days, rested on the seventh day and successfully created the Earth with its beauty. How can anyone who wants to start a business, or any group of people in a nation, work an average of three to four days a week and expect to become outstandingly productive and successful.

Day 239

Your ideas may fail but that does not necessarily mean you have failed. Because you have every opportunity to start again from experience this time around.

Day 240

Until your dreams becomes scary to you, and to your friends and family who think you are crazy, you are not an entrepreneur.

Day 241

A person can strive for perfection with almost no impact on being excellent. Perfection is about being flawless. Excellence is about doing something very well to the point of being outstanding. Each one of us has a responsibility to task ourselves with being the best in what we do to deliver quality and to become excellent at it.

Day 242

Until you believe in yourself and your idea, your business will struggle to get established and gain its market share.

Day 243

Planning is good but do more than just plan. Without action you lose momentum and end up with dead dreams.

Day 244

Until you are willing to follow through with what you learnt, you are just accumulating information.

Day 245

What differentiates entrepreneurs from everyone else is their inability to dither on an idea. They follow through with actionable steps much faster than everyone else.

Day 246

Your success hinges on two things; you and your imagination.

Day 247

Aiming high is what gives you significant results, because it enables you to expand your thinking and drives you in the direction of possibilities.

Day 248

If God speaks to you, impress on your heart, give you a better solution to a problem and cause you to perceive an opportunity or dream about a concept, it is your responsibility to research it, seek expert advice and put a plan together for Him to provide the resources to execute it and turn it into a successful business.

Day 249

Have you heard the saying 'God helps those who help themselves' Do not subscribe to that. Be of the view that 'God helps those who take action and responsibility for their part in the process.'

Day 250

True intentions always win in the end. Let that be your guide on your business journey.

Day 251

Visualisation is the seed of dreams. Until you can see it with your inner eye, it is difficult to dream about it.

Day 252

Poverty, lack and perpetual insufficiency do not glorify God. Neither does hiding behind God and doing nothing. What glorifies Him, among other things, is stepping out, creating businesses and prospering to His glory. Because God delights in the prosperity of His servants.

Day 253

Feed your faith now without apology because faith is necessary to navigate and survive life successfully. Faith is essential to start, run and grow a successful business. Whichever way you choose to look at it, faith must be a solid and constant at all times for a believer to successfully navigate life and business. Faced with the choice Don't hesitate to go for faith.

Day 254

When you take out action out of the equation after praying, you only end up operating outside the realm of faith.

Day 255

When you've been through the 'mill of life' and been really pressed, you don't see achievements as personal accomplishments, even though others may see it that way.

Day 256

An individual or community who is not prepared or willing to sacrifice today for value tomorrow is set for a prolonged, unpleasant struggle.

Day 257

It is often said 'waiting is not in vain'. However, that is guaranteed when you take advantage of the waiting period to perfect your act, polish your skills, set yourself upright and develop the right systems and structures as a business owner, thus ensuring that you are ready when the curtain goes up for you to take the stage.

Day 258

Never apologise for anything that does not add or bring value to your life. It's simply not worth the effort.

Day 259

A person can only be confident and feel superior over life's situations if they think superior, aspire to a superior status and work towards maintaining superior taste and standards.

Day 260

To succeed in business, you must be prepared for the risks and challenges that come with it.

Day 261

Knowing your purpose in life gives you focus. Focus means less distraction. Less distraction brings you an increase in productivity. Increased productivity translates into success.

Day 262

In business, your best is not enough without adequate knowledge of the industry, right strategies, expert advice and smart actions.

Day 263

What doesn't make sense to you is a revelation to someone else. It is in your interest to be smart and stop looking at everything only from your perspective.

Day 264

Good reputation is necessary for business success. A good reputation comes from higher service standards, quality products, consistency in delivery, and availability to the customer.

Day 265

The opportunity to prepare for anything in life is a luxury you cannot afford to lose. Unfortunately, it almost always comes unannounced.

Day 266

If the reason for doing what you do is weak, you are more likely to produce weak results and may be tempted to give up at the smallest hurdle.

Day 267

No dream is realised in a day, especially if it is of God. Preparation, time and process are essential requirements for manifestation, all of which work better with a dose of patience.

Day 268

Motives still count, even in business. They can be the difference between winning over a client, a contract or a supplier!

Day 269

If you don't approach life like a business, there will be too little to show at the end of your journey.

Day 270

A person who does not know how and when to 'shut up' by themselves, often becomes a threat to themselves and their destiny.

Day 271

You can easily know the level of a person's depth of understanding and knowledge by the questions they ask.

Day 272

Clients and customers often tend to treat you based on how they see you do business. Do not compromise on conducting yourself professionally.

Day 273

A person motivated by immediate hunger pangs tends to be easily corrupted at the smallest opportunity.

Day 274

Even if an individual has been assigned to your journey in life, you have a responsibility to manage your expectations of them. This includes friends and those around you.

Day 275

Smart people don't cut corners because cutting corners only makes the journey longer in the long run.

Day 276

A community, group of people or individuals with economic power cannot be easily overlooked, let alone ignored.

Day 277

Your destiny, assignment, calling and purpose in life should dictate the choices you make daily, weekly, monthly and yearly.

Day 278

Don't get bogged down in the end result. It is the process that has all the secrets you need to learn from.

Day 279

To be a trendsetter is much better and more rewarding than being a trend follower, both in life and in business.

Day 280

Compromising to fit in
is one of the greatest
fallacies in life because you
lose your uniqueness and
become a liar to yourself.

Day 281

Ideas rule the world. Not debates and arguments.

Day 282

It is not enough to change your mindset but to think of what it could be. Because possibilities are your greatest driving force.

Day 283

Don't give up. It won't necessarily be easy, but it will be rewarding in the end.

Day 284

God has a plan. So should you. Because nothing significant can be achieved in life or business without one.

Day 285

A good plan should help you clearly articulate the why, what, how and when to take the right actions to fulfil your dream.

Day 286

Life can only be lived successfully if you do better than average. It's the only way to stand out and make a bigger impact.

Day 287

Success is not attained by chance but is a product of consistent and persistent action in the direction of your vision, with a significant amount of passion.

Day 288

Success can come in different forms and levels, but the principles behind it are one and the same.

Day 289

Every God-given gift
comes in a raw package.
Deliberate perfecting brings
it to the level of excellence
necessary for success.

Day 290

Success is within your reach, if only you will do what is asked of you, which is to be the best at what you do and never give up doing it.

Day 291

God does not expect you to be diligent, excellent and successful if He hasn't put that ability already inside you.

Day 292

Good foundations are prerequisites for lasting success. Poor quality foundations offer you the opposite. Think about that.

Day 293

The desire to succeed is not a guarantee of becoming successful. It is the steps and action you take that guarantees success.

Day 294

Focus on doing what you love, do it well and you will achieve success.

Day 295

Achievers are self-motivators often spurred on by an inner drive for success.

Day 296

It is not smart to jump before thinking. Wisdom dictates that you 'think before the jump'. Guess why the head is at the top and the legs beneath.

Day 297

To thrive in life, think before you talk, look before you leap, plan before you act and watch before you pray.

Day 298

What you make time for says a lot, if not everything, about where you are going in life.

Day 299

True success eludes those
who have less appreciation
of the value of time.

Day 300

Time is a master tester.
It proves the depth, the
quality and the substance
of friendships, true
intentions and a person's
strength in the long run.

Day 301

Your uniqueness is a potentially outstanding ability the world is yet to see.

Day 302

Your differentiation in life is in what you know and what you do with what you know.

Day 303

Wisdom is measured by wise actions, not just wise words.

Day 304

Wisdom will offer you freely what experience will charge a great price to teach you.

Day 305

Creating customer value must be a key element in any business offering. One of the smartest ways to win customers involves a basic understanding of how to create an offering that customers value more than what the competition is offering.

Day 306

Every invention is precipitated by the question, Why can't?, Why not?, How about?, And of course the 'chance discoveries' that pop up every now and then from an original research focus.

Day 307

Innovation starts
with seeing change
as an opportunity,
not a threat.

Day 308

It is only a fool who doesn't change his mind in the face of more accurate facts, good counsel and quality information.

Day 309

It is basic wisdom to offer the very best in life and to do the right thing at every opportunity, especially if you expect the same of others. Until then, you have no right to demand of others what you are not willing to give them.

Day 310

You can never go wrong with a business idea that solves a problem if there is a gap somewhere that needs filling. Just make sure the market size is sufficient to enable you, at least, to stay around for a while.

Day 311

Choosing to develop yourself is a sign you believe you have the capacity to become better and do better.

Day 312

Discipline, like integrity is
a great asset in business.
However, it can only work
for you when you practice
and live by it consistently.

Day 313

The thing about challenges in life is that, what one person looks at and cries 'Obstacle! Problem! Impossible!' another shouts 'Opportunity! Potential! Advantage!' It all comes down to perspective. Failing to see this can rob you of so much.

Day 314

To complain only makes you keep dwelling on the problem without freeing the mind to think through potential solutions. Be wise. Free the mind to generate the solution you require.

Day 315

Being satisfied with too little is an enemy to growth and expansion.

Day 316

Getting your network, subscribers and visitors to engage, and consistency in what works best for your business, are keys to a successful social media strategy.

Day 317

People who make things happen are driven by their vision and dreams and not by the help they can get from others or the availability of the right conditions and support. Because often, they have to make the things happen. That is what makes them achievers.

Day 318

Refusing to manage one's expectation of the time it takes to attain success in business is one of the major causes of business failures within the first 2-3 years.

Day 319

Want to save a lot of money, stress and time Think of value instead of cost when working with a coach.

Day 320

Never over-promise and under-deliver in business. It has never been a clever strategy if you are in business for the long haul.

Day 321

Using a good business coach will help build your confidence, develop a winning mentality, bring clarity to your vision and challenge you to step out of your comfort zone.

Day 322

A good business coach will not be afraid to question your choices and help you find smarter ways of doing business.

Day 323

Economic downturns are among the most notorious periods for the birthing of great ideas, you just need to adjust your perspective.

Day 324

The mind's ability to be effectively creative is at its full function when consistently focused on one goal.

Day 325

Your distinction in business is as important as the quality of products and services you deliver. It is the way to sustain con¬sistent and successful growth.

Day 326

When your recruitment criteria and objectives are flawed, they reflect on the dedication and commitment of your employees.

Day 327

Opportunities in business are not always given, they are taken. That is simply the fact. Better get used to it.

Day 328

Wealth is knowledge. When shared, the secrets become known to others. Spread the word.

Day 329

In business what your connections cannot do for you, your diligence and excellence will secure for you.

Day 330

Don't exaggerate the size of the potential failure so that it paralyses you from stepping up and stepping forward.

Day 331

Innovators ask the questions 'What if ...', 'Why not ...', 'When can ...', 'How can ...', And they don't stop there but move a step further to seek ways to answer the questions.

Day 332

Your average investor is smarter than you think. Focus on building a solid case that makes you and your business attractive and you will win them over.

Day 333

Effective marketing
is registering in the
customer's mind that you
are not easily replaceable.

- -

- -

- -

- -

- -

Day 334

It is good practice to always acknowledge the talents, skills, innovation and great things others are doing. Encouraging and supporting them qualifies you for your own success.

Day 335

In this era of social media 'likes', comments and share buttons, there shouldn't be secret admirers. If someone supports your vision, encourage them to show it.

Day 336

Polished skills with quality service or products, good strategy and great presentation, is a deal breaker when pitching to investors.

Discipline is attractive. Make conscious efforts to take steps and actions that add great value to your spiritual health and growth.

Day 338

A poverty mentality makes you feel as though you must have it NOW, with no appreciation for the process. It makes you give up easily!

Day 339

You cannot fulfil purpose without a vision, goal, objective, passion, commitment and consistency. PERIOD!

Day 340

Your purpose can only be fulfilled with a healthy body, sound and informed mind, focused vision, developed skills and determination.

Day 341

You can't fulfil your purpose by constantly focusing on the negative and what you perceive as being done against you by your enemies.

Day 342

Purpose is meaningless if it is focused on you. It is best served by focusing on others and society.

Day 343

A poverty mentality makes you feel as though you can do everything by yourself, without appreciation for others' input, professional contribution and ideas!

Day 344

No matter how good
your intentions are, if your
priorities are not right,
success will be hard to
come by.

Day 345

Never compromise your values for anything, especially short gains. Because ultimately, your values are what set you apart.

Day 346

God does not give little dreams. Always remember, if He gave you that dream, be ready to walk alone at some point.

Day 347

When you fall in love with knowledge and pursue it consistently, intelligence will become your trademark.

Day 348

If something is worth believing in, go for it without hesitation. Because doubt will rob you of the motivation and determination required to make it a success.

Day 349

The size of your goal counts. Smaller goals can cause you to give up at the most insignificant hurdle. Dream BIG!

Day 350

Solution providers often command more value than problem makers.

Day 351

Standards are critical and essential landmarks for our development and growth. Without them, schools, organisations, businesses, and individuals would not achieve any goals.

Day 352

All great achievements in life are the results of setting standards above the norm.

Day 353

It is only by admiring and aiming for higher standards that we become successful.

Day 354

Standards are your friend when fulfilling your dreams, becoming a person of influence and impacting lives.

Day 355

Hating and speaking against people with higher standards is often a mark of non-achievers and average people.

Day 356

There is always the temptation to think you know it all. Never fall for it. There is always a smarter way of doing business!

Day 357

The advice of a business coach stays with you forever. The mistakes you avoid save you precious time and money. Be smart!

Day 358

A good strategy defines the nature, direction and value system of the business as an entity.

Day 359

You can only grow if you are willing to learn. The more you learn, the more you grow. You cannot change without learning.

Day 360

What you invest in informs your decisions. And your decisions are a reflection of what you choose to associate with.

Day 361

A dream gives birth
to passion and passion
produces action. Your work
ethic, consistency and
determination will deliver
excellent results.

Day 362

Success is always linked to opportunity, diligence and consistency. These are keys you cannot do without.

Day 363

Wisdom is great, but without understanding and knowledge it won't do much for you!

Day 364

If you have a poor mentality, no amount of cash will change your circumstances. Mentality is everything.

Day 365

Every problem is an opportunity to become better, to know better and to do better.

INDEX

Birthing Entrepreneurs in a Pandemic
Economy to Create Successful
Businesses and New Wealth

— OPPORTUNITIES IN THE —

NEW
ECONOMY
AND BEYOND

VICTOR KWEGYIR
Entrepreneur,
Business Consultant,
Coach & Speaker

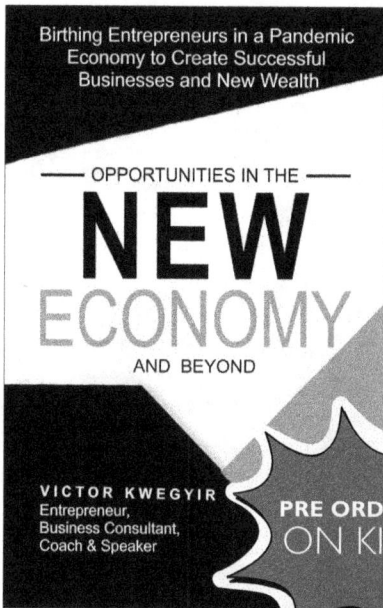

PRE ORDER NOW
ON KINDLE

ALSO AVAILABLE ON

For business coaching or help to publish your book, contact us via:
admin@victorkwegyir.com | admin@vikesprings.com

Connect with author:

/victorkwegyir   /VictorKwegyir   /victorkwegyir   @vikek

Websites: www.victorkwegyir.com   www.vikesprings.com

OTHER PUBLICATIONS

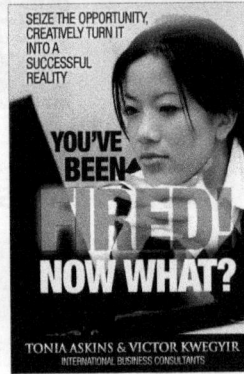

VICTOR KWEGYIR – MSc
INTERNATIONAL BUSINESS CONSULTANT, COACH & SPEAKER

PITCH YOUR BUSINESS LIKE A PRO

MASTERING THE ART OF WINNING INVESTOR
SUPPORT FOR BUSINESS SUCCESS

SIX KEY STEPS

A Handy Book For A Smart Successful Start

The **BUSINESS**
YOU CAN START

Spotting
The Greatest
Opportunities
In The Economic
Downturn

VICTOR KWEGYIR

Workbook

The **BUSINESS**
YOU CAN START

PRACTICAL EXERCISES
FOR GETTING YOU
STARTED IN BUSINESS

CREATING THE GREATEST
OPPORTUNITIES FOR A
SUCCESSFUL BUSINESS

VICTOR KWEGYIR MSc
International Business Coach & Consultant

FOLLOWING YOUR PASSION' CAN BE DECEPTIVE...

BEYOND THE PASSION

WHAT IT TAKES TO ACHIEVE
SUCCESS IN BUSINESS

VICTOR KWEGYIR
INTERNATIONAL BUSINESS CONSULTANT, COACH AND SPEAKER

OVER 250 BUSINESS QUOTES

Victor Kwegyir
International Business Consultant,
Coach, Mentor & Speaker

QUOTABLE QUOTES FOR BUSINESS

LESSONS FOR SUCCESS

SEIZE THE OPPORTUNITY,
CREATIVELY TURN IT
INTO A
SUCCESSFUL
REALITY

YOU'VE BEEN HIRED! NOW WHAT?

TONIA ASKINS & VICTOR KWEGYIR
INTERNATIONAL BUSINESS CONSULTANTS

AVAILABLE WORLDWIDE

amazon kindle

BARNES & NOBLE
BOOKSELLERS

INGRAM MICRO

Smashwords

kobo

SCRIBD

Get it on
Apple Books

available at
amazon

Available on the
iBookstore

Gardners